The Road to the Cross

Hidden Pictures Activity Book

Written by Robin Loisch

Illustrated by Marcela Gomez

warner press KiDs

305800214563

Jesus prays in the Garden of Gethsemane.

Matthew 26:36–46, Mark 14:32–42, Luke 22:39–46

Answers available @ **warnerpress.org/answer-key-E4873**

Jesus is betrayed by Judas, one of His disciples.

Matthew 26:47–50, Mark 14:43–46, Luke 22:47–53, John 18:1–11

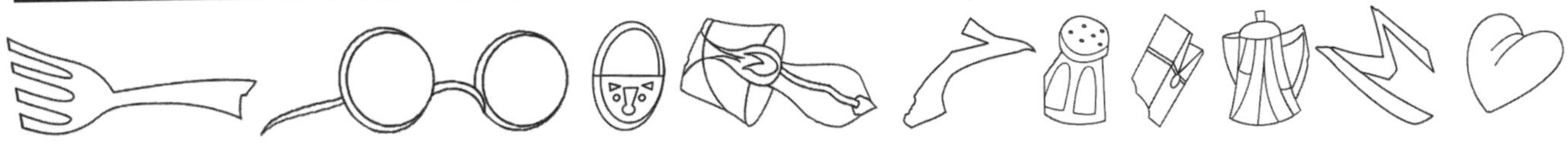

Answers available @ **warnerpress.org/answer-key-E4873**

Jesus is condemned to death by the Sanhedrin, the religious leaders of the Jews.

Matthew 27:1–2, Mark 15:1, Luke 22:66–71

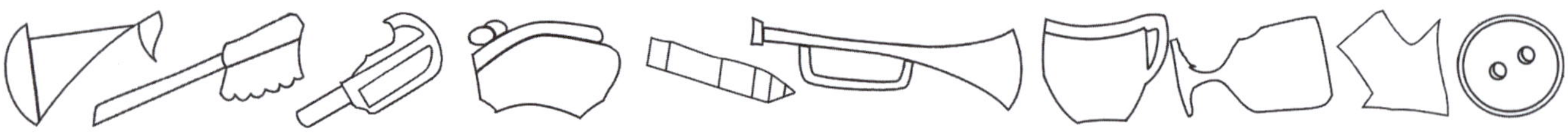

Answers available @ **warnerpress.org/answer-key-E4873**

Jesus is denied by Peter three times.

Matthew 26:69–75, Mark 14:66–72, Luke 22:54–65, John 18:25–27

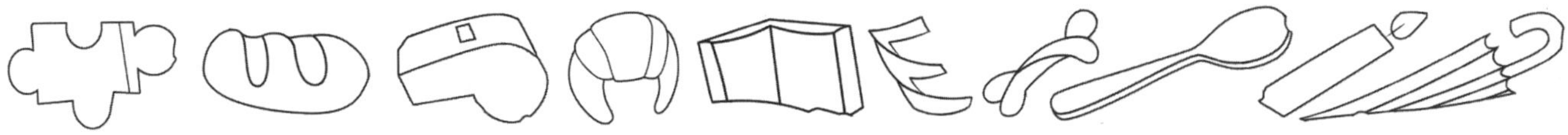

Jesus is judged by Pilate, a Roman governor.

Matthew 27:11–26, Mark 15:1–5, 15; Luke 23:1–25, John 18:28–40

Answers available @ **warnerpress.org/answer-key-E4873**

Jesus is beaten with whips and crowned with thorns.

Matthew 27:27–31, Mark 15:16–20, John 19:1–3

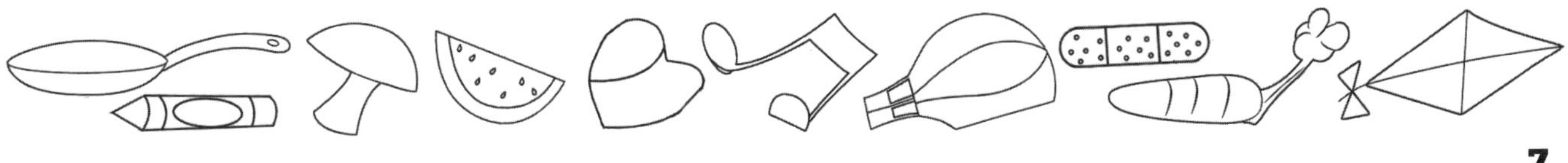

Jesus carries His cross to Golgotha, "the place of the skull."

John 19:17

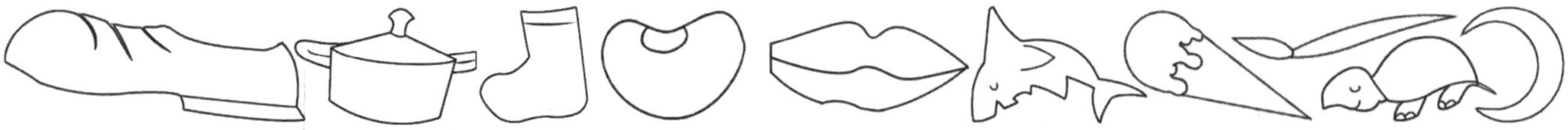

Answers available @ **warnerpress.org/answer-key-E4873**

Jesus is helped by Simon of Cyrene to carry the cross.

Matthew 27:32, Mark 15:21, Luke 23:26

Answers available @ **warnerpress.org/answer-key-E4873**

Jesus meets the women of Jerusalem, who were weeping over Him.

Luke 23:27–31

Answers available @ **warnerpress.org/answer-key-E4873**

Jesus is crucified.

Matthew 27:33–37, Mark 15:22–26, Luke 23:33–34, John 19:18–24

Jesus promises the good thief a place with Him in paradise.

Luke 23:39–43

Answers available @ **warnerpress.org/answer-key-E4873**

Jesus places His mother in the disciple John's care.

John 19:25–27

Answers available @ **warnerpress.org/answer-key-E4873**

Jesus dies on the cross to save people from their sins.

Matthew 27:45–50, Mark 15:33–37, Luke 23:44–46, John 19:28–30

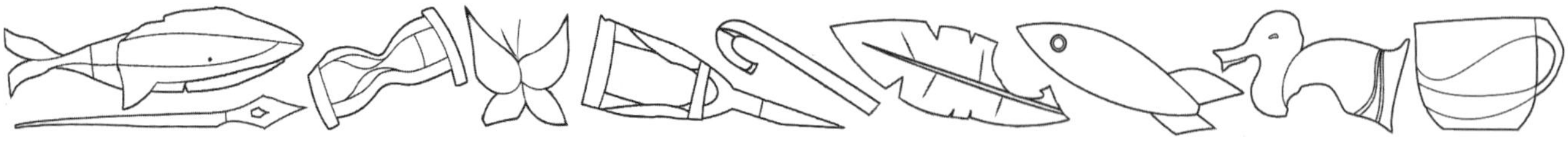

Answers available @ **warnerpress.org/answer-key-E4873**

Jesus is placed in the tomb.

Matthew 27:57–60, Mark 15:42–46, Luke 23:50–54, John 19:38–42

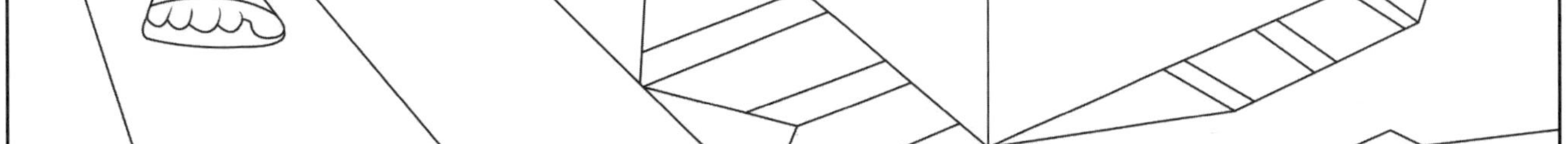

Jesus rises from the dead, offering everlasting life
to everyone who believes in Him!

Matthew 28:1–10, Mark 16:1–8, Luke 24:1–12, John 20:1–10

Answers available @ **warnerpress.org/answer-key-E4873**